The Influence of Religion on Law

ABOUT THE AUTHORS

David Kilgour is a distinguished Parliamentarian, first elected in 1979, and presently Deputy Speaker in the Canadian House of Commons. He is a graduate of the Universities of Manitoba and Toronto, and has done additional graduate work at the University of Paris. He is the author of three books—*Uneasy Patriots* (1988), *Inside Outer Canada* (1990), and *Betrayal: The Spy Canada Abandoned* (1994).

Lord Denning, "the greatest and most colourful judge this century has known," is a graduate and Hon. Fellow of Magdalen College, Oxford University and the Inns of Court. His legal career began in 1923 when he was called to the Bar in Lincoln's Inn. He became a Judge of the High Court of Justice in 1944; Lord Justice of Appeal 1948 - 57; Lord of Appeal in Ordinary 1957 - 62; and Master of Rolls 1962 - 82. He became a Bencher of Lincoln's Inn in 1944, and Treasurer of Lincoln's Inn in 1964.

He became an Hon. Bencher, Middle Temple in 1972, Gray's Inn in 1979, and Inner Temple in 1982. He has received honorary doctorates from many universities, including his alma mater, Oxford, Ottawa, Dalhousie, and Columbia Universities. Lord Denning is an Honorary Fellow of the British Academy.

His many books include *The Changing Law* (1953), *The Road to Justice* (1955), *The Discipline of Law* (1979), *The Due Process of Law* (1980), *What's Next in the Law* (1982), and *Landmarks in the Law* (1984).

Lord Denning was President of the Lawyers' Christian Fellowship (U.K.) from 1950 - 1987, and now is the Patron. *The Influence of Religion on Law* is an address which he gave to the Fellowship on the occasion of its Centenary.

The Influence of Religion on Law

by the Rt. Hon. Lord Denning
Introduction by David Kilgour, M.P.

First Canadian Edition, June 1997

© 1997 Canadian Institute for Law, Theology & Public Policy Inc.
© 1997 "The Influence of Religion on Law" by the Lawyers' Christian Fellowship, (U.K.)

Denning, Lord 1899-

    Influence of Religion on Law, The.

    ISBN 1-896363-08-3

1. Denning, Lord, 1899-
2. Jurisprudence
3. Law—Philosophy
4. Christianity and Law
5. Law and the Bible

I. Title.

Cover © Ralph Sallon

All rights reserved. No part of this work covered by the copyrights hereon may be reproduced in any form or by any means - graphic, electronic, or mechanical - without the prior written permission of the publisher.

Publisher.
Canadian Institute for Law, Theology, and Public Policy, Inc.
7203 - 90 Avenue
Edmonton, Alberta, Canada
T6B 0P5

Printed and bound in Canada by Doppler and Son

CONTENTS

Introduction 7

Influence of Religion on Law 17
    Truth 19
    "Pious Fraud" 21
    The Taking of an Oath 22
    No Half-Truths 24
    Good Faith 25
    Standard Contracts 26
    The Letter Killeth 28
    "Love Thy Neighbour" 30
    The Judge's Answer 32
    Basis of Civil Wrongs 34
    Punishment for Crime 36
    Individual Responsibility 38
    The Guilty Mind 39
    Insanity and Crime 40
    The McNaghten Rules 42
    The Straffen Case 43
    A Problem of Ethics 45
    Man and the State 47
    The Case of James I 48
    The Perils of Individualism 50
    The Influence of Christianity 52
    Family Life 54
    Change 56
    Conclusion 57

INTRODUCTION

It is a privilege to offer some introductory thoughts on an essay of major importance by probably the most important British judge of the Twentieth Century. As Master of the Rolls of the Court of Appeal in England and Wales, Lord Denning was in the unique position to shape the interpretation of the law both there and abroad. By selecting the cases to be heard, he was able to deliver far-reaching and influential decisions on many issues he judged to be in need of clarification and review. He gave many important common law judgements in a long career. Few jurists are better qualified to speak about the development of the common law in his native country and by implication in Canada as well.

From a family of modest means, Denning was educated at a grammar school in Andover, Hampshire, England, from which he progressed to Magdalen College, Oxford. He achieved highest honours in mathematics and jurisprudence, and was recognized as a most promising student in the study of law at Oxford. He joined a set of chambers in 1923, soon after he was called to the Bar, and worked on building his own practice, mostly in civil cases. He was appointed King's Counsel in 1938, and almost immediately became the legal adviser to a Regional Commissioner soon after the outbreak of World War II.

Denning received his first appointment to the bench in March 1944, having been elevated to the Probate, Divorce and Admiralty Division. He was presumably not entirely pleased with this; he noted that the court "was considered inferior and unpleasant."[1] He served there for eighteen months; he was then transferred by the post-War Labour government to the King's Bench Division, dealing with both criminal and civil matters. Promoted to the Court of Appeal in October 1946, he found himself within an institution which concentrated exclusively on civil cases until 1967, when criminal appeals also began to be heard. In 1957, Denning was appointed to the House of Lords, and served as a Law Lord in that chamber. In 1962, he was appointed as Master of the Rolls, a position that he held until 1982. In this role, he presided over and controlled the cases heard within the Civil Division of the Court of Appeal. The Court of Appeal is usually the final court of appeal in England and Wales, and hears many more cases annually than does the House of Lords. In most matters, it is the final court of appeal within England and Wales. Denning's position provided a unique opportunity to shape and mould the interpretation of law within his philosophy of how law, morality, religion, ethics, and justice should interact.

---

[1] Lowell, J.L., and J.P.W.B. McAuslan. *Lord Denning: the Judge and the Law*. (London: Sweet & Maxwell, Ltd., 1984), p. 5.

Some of the major, and significant themes in Denning's essay include:

- The interdependence of law, religion and ethics both today and in the past, with many of the most fundamental principles of law being derived from Christianity. Where religion and law interact is through the rulings of judges that have been brought up in the Christian faith. "The precepts of religion, consciously or unconsciously, have been their guide in the administration of justice," says Denning.

For example, the principle of love for one's neighbour is one of the fundamental guiding forces in the administration of justice. Denning's view of justice is fixed by one of the most fundamental precepts of the Christian faith, i.e., love for one's neighbour. The corollary to this, of course, is that "The rule that you are to love your neighbour becomes in law you must not injure your neighbour." The principle that was derived from this in English common law is that of 'reasonable forseeability.' It reasons that a person must take care to avoid acts or omissions that are likely to injure neighbours. Civil damages for negligent acts are meant to act as compensation for an injured neighbour, not a means of punishment against transgressors.

There is, however, a distinction between the notion of compensation for a civil wrong and the principle of punishment for a criminal wrong. Denning espouses the view that it is society that creates the conditions that make people criminals, and that the best way to deal with crime is to reform society itself. It is important to note that there is an onus on the individual to reform and repent; there can be no excuse for one's behaviour due to his or her situation in society. While Christianity stresses the responsibility of the individual for behaviour, it also stresses the need for penitence on the part of individuals.

Concepts of individual responsibility do not adequately address the issue of insanity for defendants in criminal cases. In the event of an insanity plea, much of the decision rests with the jury; it is they who must decide whether or not to convict. This decision by the jury must take into account the state of the accused's mind at the moment of the impugned act.

The institution of marriage remains vital in virtually all countries The ease by which divorce is granted in modern times often leads the parties to disregard the consequences for their children. Denning writes: ". . . if the law fails to uphold the institution of marriage, how can we expect young people to do so . . . . This development is undermining the institution of the family, and the whole fabric of society." He makes this point, not to endorse the tightening of the divorce laws; instead he believes that the interpretations of law made in the nineteenth century are not suited to the "social necessities and social opinion" that exists in the present one. He exhorts believer jurists to use their influence to aid Parliament in the remoulding and reshaping of laws to meet the realities of the present day.

- ◆ The importance of absolute truth both in Christianity and the courts. Without binding oaths and unvarnished truth by witnesses, trial justice becomes essentially impossible. Denning discusses half-truths at some length from the standpoint of a believer jurist. Without religion, a witness is likely to say in court or elsewhere only what helps their cause, whether true or false. He discounts the notion of "pious fraud," which is employed as a form of half-truth. Denning's low regard for half-truths assumes that the law is just; in a system where law is unjust, "pious frauds" may be excused.

  The issue of law being derived from religion is a core assumption of Denning's writing. The rule of English common law is that without a guilty mind, guilt does not exist. A punishable act must be one that is morally deserving of blame, i.e., it must be a sin. In the same vein, the truth must be ascertained for justice to be served. To be as certain as possible that the truth is disclosed, the oath that witnesses take binds their conscience to their religion. Denning notes that there is nothing that illustrates the impact of religion on law as clearly as the taking of the witnesses' oath. He argues that the perceived decline of honesty in society is perhaps due to the decline of the role of religion; people are increasingly disposed to disclose only those facts which help their cause.

♦ In contracts, where Denning is an acknowledged world expert, he reminds us that today if one makes a promise intended to be binding and to be acted upon by the person to whom it is directed, it becomes enforceable in law once the other has acted upon it. He criticizes the current common law practice of holding a contract enforceable even if unpredictable circumstances arise which render it impossible to enforce it, citing St. Thomas Aquinas who would excuse a contractor in such circumstances. Similarly with statutes, Denning thinks a literal interpretation of their letter has superseded an interpretation of the spirit of the words. He notes that it is not for the judiciary "to fill in the gaps in the acts of Parliament."

This view, however, should not be construed as an endorsement of a passive judiciary, one that does not take an active role in the formulation of policies that further the principle of justice. He espouses the view that judges should not be reduced to a 'sterile' role of interpreting existing and outmoded statutes, but should "develop the law case by case . . . so that the litigants . . . can have their differences decided by the law as it should be and is . . . not by the law of the past."[2] In this vein, Denning demonstrates a healthy scepticism for precedent, and has never felt restrained from creating his own interpretation of the law. Denning's view, however, is that he would prefer a judiciary that is required to undertake such interpretations as infrequently as possible. His prescription for remedying such situations would be for acts of Parliament to be written in as plain a language as possible. "To my mind, the one way to get it straight is for Parliament to use plain, simple language expressing principles, and for the judges to fill in the gaps in a statute so as to do what good sense requires."[3]

Denning asserts that it is the spirit, not the letter of a contract or law, that should be followed. He warns against the literal interpretation of statutes or contracts, saying that, "It makes words the masters of men instead of their servants." In early English jurisprudence, justices interpreted laws and statutes in the spirit in which Parliament intended them to function, thus eliminating the problems of unforeseen events and areas which the law was not intended to address. This practice was abandoned in the Nineteenth Century, when statutes were interpreted

---

[2] Robson, Peter and Paul Watchman. *Justice, Lord Denning and the Constitution*. (Westmead, Farnborough, England: Gower Publishing Co., Ltd., 1981), p. 2.
[3] Denning, The Rt Hon Lord. *The Closing Chapter*. (London: Butterworth & Co., 1983), p. 112.

according to the "grammatical and ordinary sense of the words." Denning concludes that judges should seek to interpret statutes in a reasonable way, even if this involves a departure from the letter of the law. "By doing so, they are more likely to find the truth," he argues.

- The individual is of primary importance, not society. States have no ultimate authority of their own, but derive all their authority from God.

The notion that "The King is under God and the law" affirms the subordination of the state to belief. This affirmation simply illustrates the Christian principle written by St. Paul in his letter to the Romans: "There is no power but God: The powers that be are ordained by God." The individual is the unit that carries worth, while society is simply a creature of the collective decisions of individuals. The paramountcy of the individual is a principal tenet of Christian ethics. This paramountcy of the individual should not be construed as a concomitant endorsement of the notion of unfettered material accumulation, without regard for the effect on others. While the pursuit of wealth itself is not necessarily undesirable, no one should forget that is only through society that wealth is acquired and amassed.

The interpretations of the law by Lord Denning in his long and distinguished career have shaped not only the way law is applied, but also how it is perceived. In this article, Denning raises the issue of how society has taken religion and belief and incorporated it into our legal systems. While these systems are different in many respects across regions, the common thread across so many of them is that their core values are derived from the tenets of religion. During his lengthy tenure, Denning has increased that awareness of the impact of religion on law. As lawyers, judges, members of the public and legislators, we should recognize the central role that belief holds in our systems of jurisprudence. During his lifetime, Lord Denning has articulated, shaped, and defined our system of law to reflect not only our humanity, but our spirituality as well.

David Kilgour*
Ottawa, February 1997

* I must acknowledge the contribution of James Jordan, a student at the Center for the Study of Canada at the State University of New York at Plattsburgh. Mr. Jordan is currently serving as an intern in my Ottawa office.

THE INFLUENCE OF RELIGION ON LAW

by the Rt. Hon. Lord Denning

In primitive societies the influence of religion on law was obvious, but it is not so obvious in modern societies. In primitive communities religion, morals and law were indistinguishably mixed together. In the Ten Commandments, for instance, you find the First Commandment, which is religious: "God spake these words and said, 'I am the Lord thy God: Thou shalt have none other Gods but me.'" You find the Fifth Commandment, which is a moral precept: "Honour thy father and thy mother, that thy days may be long in the land which the Lord thy God giveth thee." You find the Eighth Commandment, which is a legal duty: "Thou shalt not steal." This intermingling is typical of all early communities. The severance of these ideas—of law from morality, and of religion from law — belongs very distinctly to the later stages of the evolution of modern thought.

This severance has gone a great way. Many people now think that religion and law have nothing in common. The law, they say, governs our dealings with our fellows, whereas religion concerns our dealings with God. Likewise, they hold that law has nothing to do with morality. Law lays down rigid rules which must be obeyed without questioning whether they are right or wrong. Its function is to keep order, not to do justice.

The severance has, I think, gone much too far. Although religion, law and morals can be separated, they are nevertheless still very much dependent on one another. Without religion, there can be no morality, there can be no law. I shall try to show you how many of the fundamental principles of our law have been derived from the Christian religion. In so doing I will try to indicate how they are challenged by a changing world which knows no religion, or which at best treats religion as something which is of no moment in practical affairs.

TRUTH

Let me start first with Truth. No one reading this doubts, I hope, that it is your duty to tell the truth. Nevertheless, if your actions were governed by expediency alone, without regard to the precepts of law, religion or morals, you would soon find that there is as much to be said for lying as there is for telling the truth. You would discard the old saying that "honesty is the best policy" as a maxim fit for fools, but not for clever people like yourself. If it were necessary, in order to attain your ends, that you should tell a lie, then tell it you would, for the end would justify the means. For instance, if your friend were charged with being drunk in charge of a car, and it would help him for you to say that he was sober, then say it you would, although you knew he was drunk.

The reason why that reasoning is not acceptable to most of us, I believe, is because we have been taught the contrary from our mothers' knees. The Christian religion has always stressed the importance of truth, absolute truth, in all our dealings. Just as the psalmist commends the man who "speaketh the truth from his heart" (Psalms 15:2) so also St. Paul enjoins the early Christians in these words: "Wherefore putting away lying, speak every man truth with his neighbour, for we are members one of another" (Ephesians 4:25). If there is one thing that gives rise to more resentment than anything else, it is to be deceived, to be told a lie. It is an affront to the whole personality. Just as we do not wish others to deceive us, so we should not deceive them.

"PIOUS FRAUD"

Some theologians have argued that it is permissible to tell a lie for a just cause. A part of the Church itself did so at one time. For instance, they invented legendary incidents relating to the life of Our Lord and the saints, and portrayed them as true. It was done with the best of motives so as to help people to believe, but nevertheless it was a fraud. Hence the phrase "pious fraud," which has become part of our language. A parallel in modern times occurs when doctors sometimes deceive their patients because they believe it is for the patients' good to do so. I am not sure, however, that it is ever permissible for any man to tell a lie to his neighbour. St.Augustine held that the duty of truth is absolute and he would permit no exceptions to it. He gave as a sufficient reason that, by lying, eternal life is lost. In modern time, Kant and other philosophers take the view that truth is absolute. What then, you may ask, is to be said about stratagems made by our military men for deceiving the enemy? Some of them are downright lies, but no one sees any wrong in them. On the contrary, it is a matter for congratulation when they succeed. The answer for the Christian is, I suggest, that an enemy who is seeking to destroy you can hardly be considered your neighbour.

THE TAKING OF AN OATH

Turning now to the law, it has insisted upon the truth being told on all occasions without exception. It is not difficult to see the reason why. Justice cannot be done unless the truth be known. The Judges have to rely on the statements of witnesses. If it were permissible for a witness to tell a lie to help his friend, it would be the end of any attempt to do justice. I must remark, however, in parenthesis, that this reasoning assumes that the law itself is just, and that Judges decide the cases justly. If the law is harsh and unjust, or is unjustly administered, then witnesses may be tempted to permit themselves a "pious fraud." In the old days when stealing anything worth more than forty shillings was punishable with death, a jury solemnly found that a £5 bank note was only worth £1.95 and no one thought it reprehensible. Hence the importance of seeing that the law is not only certain, but also that it is just.

On the assumption that the law is just, the Judges insist on absolute truth, and to emphasize its importance, they require the witness to take an oath that he will tell the truth. There is nothing, perhaps, in our legal procedure which so clearly shows the influence of religion as the taking of an oath. Ever since there has been a system of law in this country, it has proceeded on the footing that each man believes in God. And it still proceeds on that footing. When a man goes into the witness box the first thing he has to do is to take the oath. Silence is demanded in Court to emphasize the solemnity of what he is about to do. The witness takes the book in his hand and says these words: "I swear by Almighty God that the evidence I shall give shall be the truth, the whole truth, and nothing but the truth." The book that is handed to him, unless he asks for another (or affirms), is the New Testament. By the oath the witness is not merely making a solemn affirmation to the Judge, he is binding himself to God that he will tell the truth, and there is no room for half-truths or pious frauds. This is well known to ordinary folk who come to give evidence. Some of the more emphatic sort have been known to protest too much the truth of their answer by adding, "May God strike me dead if I have told a lie." It is recorded that on one occasion on the Western Circuit a witness who had made such an exclamation did fall down dead. A stone is set up in the market place at Devizes to note the fact! Witnesses of other religious faiths take the oath according to the form of their own religion, but it must always be an oath which is binding on their conscience.

NO HALF-TRUTHS

So much for witnesses. But the law not only insists on people telling the truth under oath, it also insists on truth in all affairs of life where one person acts on the word of another. There is nothing upon which the law is more strict. It allows no evasions. Half-truths are condemned as much as real falsehoods. If a statement is literally true but conveys a wrong impression because of what is left unsaid, that is fraud, as the late Lord Kylsant once found out to his cost. He had inserted in a company's prospectus figures for the years which had shown profits but had omitted those for the years which had shown losses. The net result was to make the Company's position look much better than it was. He was sent to prison for twelve months. The principle underlying all the rules of the law on these subjects—fraud, misrepresentation, estoppel and the like—is this: no man shall get a benefit from a lie if the law can prevent him. No excuse or justification is permitted. It is not allowable to tell a lie in order to achieve a just result. A good end does not justify a bad means. The law, therefore, is sound enough on this point, but what I would observe is that the law is not sufficient by itself. If the people have no true religion, then all the ordinances of the law are of little use. May not this be the reason why honesty has declined in recent times? Many people do not seem nowadays to pay much regard to the sanctity of an oath. They say that which they think helps their cause, whether it be true or not.

GOOD FAITH

Akin to truth is the requirement of good faith. Just as you must tell the truth, so you must keep your promises. The just man in the Psalms is not only "he that hath used no deceit on his tongue," but also "he that sweareth unto his neighbour and disappointeth him not, though it were to his own hindrance" (Psalm 15:3-5). This precept finds its place in the law also. Our law of contract has passed through many phases. At one time promises were not binding unless they were made in the form of a covenant under seal. Later on they were not binding unless there was consideration for them, that is something given or done as the price for them. Nowadays nearly all formalities have been eliminated. If a person makes a promise which is intended to be binding and to be acted upon by the party to whom it is addressed, then once that person has acted upon it, it is enforceable at law.

STANDARD CONTRACTS

So far so good. But the law on this matter has on occasions overreached itself. The best instance is perhaps the way it has treated standardised contracts. Large concerns, such as hire-purchase companies, insurance companies, and others often issue printed forms containing many conditions of contract. The small individual member of the public has no choice but either to accept them or to go without the benefit of any contract at all. More often than not, he does not read them, and even if he did, he would probably not understand them. Yet he is in general bound by their conditions as if he had deliberately promised to fulfill them, although some exceptions have now been made by legislation to ameliorate the injustice, notably the Misrepresentation Act, 1967 and the Unfair Contract Terms Act, 1977. Again, when it comes to interpretation of contracts, the law holds the man bound to the letter of his contract, although unforeseen circumstances have arisen which make it unjust to enforce it against him. If he protests and says, "I could not have foreseen it," the law replies, "It is your own fault. You ought to have put in a saving clause to protect yourself." This harsh ruling is not in accordance with the view of St.Thomas Aquinas, who would have held him excused. If good faith is required in a person who gives a promise, so it should be in a person who takes the benefit of it. He should not enforce it in circumstances which it was never intended to cover.

Just as the law has overreached itself with contracts, so it has also with the interpretation of statutes. If a situation arises which Parliament never intended, and a strict interpretation of the statute gives rise to injustice, nevertheless the law cannot, or will not, lift a finger to help. It is not for the Judges to fill in the gaps in the Acts of Parliament.

THE LETTER KILLETH

I cannot help thinking that this literal interpretation of contracts or statutes is a departure from real truth. It makes words the masters of men instead of their servants. If you read your New Testament, you will find that there is nothing more condemned than the insistence on the letter of the law. A good instance is the case about the Sabbath day. The Fourth Commandment ordained that on it "thou shalt do no manner of work." It so happened that on one Sabbath day as the disciples went through the corn fields, they began to pluck the ears of corn. The Pharisees said to the Lord, "Why do they on the Sabbath day that which is not lawful?" He replied, "The Sabbath was made for man, and not man for the Sabbath" (St. Mark 2:23-28). St. Paul put the principle succinctly when he said, "the letter killeth but the spirit giveth life" (Corinthians 3:6). That precept was at one time remembered in our English law. In the days when the Bible was first put into English, the Judges laid down rules which were undoubtedly influenced by Biblical teaching. The statutes were to be interpreted not only according to the language used but also with regard to the mischief which Parliament sought to remedy, so as to give "force and life" to the intention of the Legislature. Those words were clearly taken from the Epistle, "the spirit giveth life." In the nineteenth century that broad view was supplanted by a rule which Baron Parke described as a golden rule. He said that statutes, and indeed all documents, were to be interpreted according to the grammatical and ordinary sense of the words. Even if the grammatical meaning gave rise to unjust results which Parliament never intended, nevertheless the grammatical meaning must prevail. This means, I fear, that the Judges are too often inclined to fold their hands and blame the Legislature, when really they ought to set to work and give the words a reasonable meaning, even if this does involve a departure from the letter of them. By so doing they are more likely to find the truth.

"LOVE THY NEIGHBOUR"

Let us now turn from Truth to Justice. No one reading this doubts, I hope, that it is his duty to be just and fair in all his dealings. But our conception of justice is only the Christian teaching of love. Such at least was the view of William Temple, Archbishop of Canterbury, one of the greatest thinkers of the present century. "It is axiomatic," he said, "that love should be the predominant Christian impulse and that the primary form of love in social organization is justice." The Christian standpoint is summed up in the Gospel when a certain lawyer asked our Lord:

> "Master, what shall I do to inherit eternal life?" He said unto him, "What is written in the law? How readest thou?" And he answering said, "Thou shalt love the Lord thy God with all thy heart, and with all thy soul and with all thy mind, and thy neighbour as thyself." And he said unto him, "Thou hast answered right: this do and thou shalt live."

This precept—love towards God and love towards yours neighbour—is a precept of religion, but nevertheless in many affairs of life, love can only find expression through justice. William Temple gave this illustration:

> Imagine a Trade Union Committee negotiating with an Employer's Federation in an in-

dustrial crisis on the verge of a strike. This Committee is to be actuated by love. Oh yes, by all means, but towards whom? Are they to love the workers or the employers? Of course—both. But then that will not help them much to determine what terms ought to be either proposed or accepted . . . . Love in fact finds its primary expression through justice which, in the field of industrial disputes, means in practice that each side should state its case as strongly as it can before the most impartial tribunal available, with determination to accept the award of that tribunal. At least that puts the two parties on a level, and it is to that extent in accordance with the command, "Thou shalt love thy neighbour as thyself."

THE JUDGE'S ANSWER

Such being the view of the theologian, now turn to the Judge whose task it is to be the tribunal. He must do justice between the parties. But how is he to know what is justice? Let me tell you how one great Judge answered the question. There was a case where a manufacturer of ginger beer had made it so carelessly that he left a snail in one of the bottles. He sold it as part of a consignment to a shopkeeper, who in turn sold a bottle to a man whose wife drank it and was injured. At one time the law held that the manufacturer was not liable to pay any compensation because he had made no contract with the ultimate purchaser or his wife. But in 1932 the House of Lords held that the manufacturer was liable. In a judgment of great importance in the law, Lord Atkin took the Christian precept as the underlying basis of the decision in these words:

> The rule that you are to love your neighbour becomes in law, "You must not injure your neighbour," and the lawyer's question, "Who is my neighbour?" receives a restricted reply. You must take reasonable care to avoid acts or omissions which you can reasonably foresee would be likely to injure your neighbour. Who then in law is my neighbour? The answer seems to be—persons who are so closely and directly affected by any act that I ought reasonably to have them in contemplation as being so affected when I am directing my

mind to the acts or omissions which are called in question. *See Donoghue v Stevenson [1932] A.C. 562, 580.*

It is, I suggest to you, a most significant thing that a great Judge should draw his principles of law, or rather his principles of justice, from the Christian commandment of love. I do not know where else he is to find them. Some people speak of natural justice as though it was a thing well recognizable by anyone, whatever his training and upbringing. But I am quite sure that our conception of it is due entirely to our habits of thought through many generations. The common law of England has been moulded for centuries by Judges who have been brought up in the Christian faith. The precepts of religion, consciously or unconsciously, have been their guide in the administration of justice.

BASIS OF CIVIL WRONGS

Perhaps the best illustration of this is the law of this country about civil wrongs. At one time the ruling principle, derived from Roman law, was that a person was not liable to pay damages unless he had been guilty of some fault, such as some negligence, some invasion on another's property, or the like. The underlying justification for this rule was that damages were a deterrent. If he was made to pay damages, he was not so likely to commit the same fault again. But those who put forward this view always had great difficulty in explaining why a master should be liable to pay damages for his servant's fault. Nowadays, save for rare exceptions, damages are not regarded as a deterrent or a punishment, but rather as compensation for harm done. The law proceeds, I suggest, on the Christian principle that if you love your neighbour, you will take care not to injure him. And if perchance you should by your negligence (or even by the negligence of your servants) do him some damage, you will wish to compensate him. If you do not do so, the law will require you to do what you ought to have done willingly, but it will not go further and punish you. It will not exact anything in the nature of vengeance or retribution. If proof of this were needed, it is to be found in the fact that you can insure yourself against any damages you have to pay. This means that the law does not insist on the compensation coming from your own pocket. It is sufficient if your insurance company pays. It is obvious that, when you have covered your liability by insurance, the award of damages has no punitive or deterrent effect on you. It is compensation for the injured party and nothing else. Once this is appreciated, you can understand why a master should pay compensation for his servant's fault. The servant is doing the master's business and the master should be answerable for the servant's act as if it were his own. A noteworthy illustration of the modern approach is to be found in the case of a guest of a Brighton Hotel who got annoyed with the manager and made a brutal assault on him. He was taken before the criminal courts and found to be insane. He could not therefore be said to be at fault, but nevertheless he was ordered by a civil court to pay compensation to the injured manager.

PUNISHMENT FOR CRIME

While civil wrongs are thus redressed by compensation, there still remain all the criminal wrongs which must be met by punishment. The command that you are to love your neighbour does not mean that those who do wrong should not be punished. In the Epistle of St. Peter it is said that governors are sent by God "for the punishment of evil-doers." What then is the right way to punish them? What is to be done with people who are enemies of society, men who prey upon it by theft and fraud, men who assault innocent women and children, men who are murderers? At one time the law held that they should be exterminated. Nearly all serious offenses were punishable by death. But under the influence of a more humane jurisprudence, or rather, I would say of a Christian outlook, capital punishment was abolished in all cases except murder and treason. Now it has for practical purposes been abolished altogether.

In any discussion of punishment it is important to recognize, as Christianity does, that society itself is responsible for the conditions which make men criminals. It is commonplace that broken homes produce juvenile delinquents. The child who has lost his sense of security feels that he must fight for his interests in a hostile world. He becomes anti-social and finally criminal. The broken home from which he comes is only too often a reflection on society itself, a society which has failed to respect the sanctity of marriage, a society which has failed to maintain its standards of morality, a society which has lost its religion. When we try to reform the criminal, we are only treating the symptoms of the disease. We are not tackling the cause of it. The best way to deal with it is to reform society itself. In this regard, I need hardly say that the leaders of society have a special responsibility. It is disturbing to find how many broken homes, how many matrimonial offenses, exist among those in high positions.

INDIVIDUAL RESPONSIBILITY

Nevertheless, although society itself is largely responsible, neither religion nor the law excuses the criminal himself. Christianity has always stressed the responsibility of each individual for his own wrongdoing. It does not say to him, "Poor thing, you couldn't help it, could you? You came from a broken home and nothing else could be expected." That would lead him to believe that he is more sinned against than sinning and implies that strenuous moral effort on his part is unnecessary or futile. The Christian approach is different. It allows no easy excuse but demands of every one that he must repent and reform. One of the opening sentences of the *Book of Common Prayer* of 1662 is, "When the wicked man turneth away from his wickedness that he hath committed, and doeth that which is lawful and right, he shall save his soul alive." As it is said in the Gospel of St. Luke, "There is joy in the presence of God over one sinner that repenteth."

THE GUILTY MIND

In order to hold a person individually responsible for his crime, so that he is liable to punishment, it is obviously necessary that he should have a guilty mind. This requirement is first found in St. Augustine's sermons, where it is said that you are not guilty of perjury unless you have a guilty mind. Thence, it found its place in the laws of Henry I, where it was laid down as law, "*Actus non facit reum, nisi mens sit rea*"; that is, there is no guilt unless there is a guilty mind. That requirement has been the rule of English common law from that time to this. In order for an act to be punishable, it must be morally blameworthy. It must be a sin. (Of course, there are special reasons for making some conduct or lack of care "absolute offenses," but these are exceptions.)

INSANITY AND CRIME

When you speak of a guilty mind, however, the question immediately arises, "How are you to deal with those who are not of sound mind?" At first sight the law seems clear enough. If a man is insane when he commits a crime, he cannot be punished, because he cannot be said to have a guilty mind. But the difficulty arises when you ask, "What is insanity?" Time and time again it used to happen that a jury would find a man guilty of willful murder while of sound mind, but nevertheless he was afterwards reprieved on the grounds that he had since been found to be insane. It was the accepted practice, authorized by statute, for the Home Secretary to appoint two doctors to examine him. If the doctors found him to be insane, he was reprieved. In theory, the finding of the doctors did not contradict the verdict of the jury. The jury was concerned only with his state of mind when he committed the crime, whereas the doctors were concerned with it at the time that they examined him. If he was insane at that time, he could not be hanged. As a matter of common sense, the findings of the jury and the doctors ought usually to have coincided. One realizes, of course, that they could differ. A man may be so mentally affected by his trial and sentence that he becomes insane afterwards, but that is a rare thing. His sanity is usually the same throughout. The reason why the Home Office doctors so often found him to be insane was that they adopted a different test of insanity from that which the jury had to apply. Let me tell you about these tests because they can both be traced to the Christian conception of individual responsibility, but each regarding it in a different light.

THE McNAGHTEN RULES

The test applied by the jury in judging insanity was the test laid down by the Judges in 1843 in the McNaghten Rules. These rules placed the emphasis on the man's knowledge, not on his will-power. If he was so made that he did not know what he was doing at all, any more than a sleep-walker does, then he was excused. Or if he did not know that what he was doing was wrong, as if he was under a delusion that he was being attacked in war by the enemy, then also he was excused. But if he knew what he was doing and that it was wrong, then he was not excused. It may be that he was driven on by some blind impulse; nevertheless, if he knew it was wrong, he was not excused in law.

The test applied by the doctors in judging insanity denied the distinction between a man's knowledge and his will-power. If the man was what they called a psychopathic personality, driven on by some morbid urge which he had not the will-power to resist, then the doctors held that he should be excused, even though he knew perfectly well that he was doing wrong.

THE STRAFFEN CASE

The difference of approach was well illustrated by two cases some years ago from the era of capital punishment. A young man called Straffen strangled two small girls. He was arrested, but when brought up for trial, the doctors said he was unfit to plead, and accordingly he was detained in the Broadmoor Asylum. He behaved himself well in the asylum, but one day he escaped for a few hours and strangled another small girl. He was again arrested and brought up for trial. This time the doctors said he was fit to plead. The defense of insanity was raised, but the jury rejected it and found him guilty of willful murder. Later he was reprieved on the ground, no doubt, that the Home Office doctors found him to be insane.

I expect that the jury reasoned something like this: "This man is better out of the way. He is subject to such dreadful impulses that it is better for the community that he should be put to death rather than there should be any risk of another escape. This should be done, not so much to punish him as to protect the community." The view of the doctors presumably was: "This man is not responsible for his actions. He is subject to impulses which he cannot resist. He should be regarded as insane and should not be punished."

In contrast to the Straffen case, there was the case of Miles Giffard, a young man who murdered both his father and his mother and pushed the bodies in a wheel-barrow over the edge of a cliff. He did it because they wouldn't let him have the use of a car or some other quite inadequate reason. He and his family had a history of mental instability. The defense of insanity was raised but the jury found him guilty. This time the Home Secretary did not grant a reprieve and Giffard was hanged. This case seems to show that there are some crimes which shock the public conscience so much that ordinary members of the public say that the murderer is better out of the way, even though he was mentally unstable. It is not so much a matter of punishing him. It is rather the community defending itself. It is said that Giffard went to his death repentant for his sins and, it may be hoped, at peace with his maker.

A PROBLEM OF ETHICS

It is worth pausing for a moment at this point because those two cases illustrate one of the most difficult problems of Christian ethics of our time. It is this: is it permissible for society to exterminate those who have an irresistible impulse to murder? A similar problem arises about sterilization. If a man is subject to mad sexual impulses which cause him to inflict grave injury on innocent women, is it permissible compulsorily to sterilise him, or alternatively to keep him in prison indefinitely until he is past the age when he will do such things? In Denmark they have a law whereby a sexual offender is sentenced to prison for as long as the State thinks fit to keep him there, but he can obtain his freedom by submitting to sterilization. In England we have never gone so far. We do not generally permit sterilization of the unfit, at least as a punishment or as a protection for society (as opposed, in very extreme cases, to it being done for the protection of a person of unsound mind against the consequences of her or his own instincts—a doubtful practice which in the last few years has crept in.[*] I expect that the refusal of the law to sterilise the offender has its origin in the sanctity which Christianity attaches to human life. Just as life itself is sacred, so are the means of producing it, and it is not to be taken away except by him who is the creator of it. The danger is, of

---

[*] Exampled by T v T, (1988) 2WLR 189, and F. West Berkshire Health Authority (*Times Newspaper*, 5 May 1989, H.L.).

course, that once authority is given to society to exterminate, to sterilise or to intern indefinitely some of its members, you may find that those who are in authority in the State may use it, as the Nazis did, against those whom they dislike. I offer no solution except to suggest that true Christianity should try to strike a correct balance between the individual and the society of which he forms a part.

MAN AND THE STATE

I have now told you all I wish of Truth and Justice: but these lead me on to consider the relations between man and the State. Truth and Justice do not exist in a vacuum. They exist in a society of human beings, in short, in a State, and a State can be so organized that Truth and Justice can disappear, or at any rate be stifled. What does Christianity say about this? Let me take for an answer again the words of William Temple: "The primary principle of Christian Ethics and Christian politics must be respect for every person simply as a person. If each man and woman is a child of God, whom God loves and for whom Christ died, then there is in each a worth absolutely independent of all usefulness to society. The person is primary, not the society: the State exists for the citizen, not the citizen for the State."

The Christian Church has always insisted that the State has no ultimate and omnipotent authority of its own but derives its authority from God. St. Paul in his Epistle to the Romans (13:1) made this clear. "There is no power but of God. The powers that be are ordained by God." This has been the shield under which our forefathers resisted oppression. To quote St. Paul again—the Ruler of the State was the "Minister of God for good," and so long as he fulfilled his high trust, it was not right to resist him, but if he forsook it and sought absolute power, then resistance was justified.

THE CASE OF JAMES I

A celebrated instance occurred when James I claimed the right to rule in England as an absolute sovereign. He claimed that he could Judge whatever he pleased in his own person, free from all risks of prohibition or appeal. He called in aid the authority of Archbishop Bancroft who declared that it was clear in divinity that he could try cases himself. Such power, said the Archbishop, doubtless belongs to the King by the word of God in the scriptures. But there was a great Lord Chief Justice in those days, Lord Coke, who made it a rule of his life to spend one-fourth of each day in prayer. I must say that I do not know how he managed it, considering the vast amount of other things that he did. Lord Coke told the King that he had no power to try cases himself, and that all cases ought to be determined in a Court of Justice. King James replied, "I always thought and I often heard the boast that your English law is founded upon reason. If that be so, why have not I and others reason as well as you the Judges?" The Lord Chief Justice replied, "True it is, please Your Majesty, that God has endowed Your Majesty with excellent science as well as great gifts of nature, but Your Majesty will allow me to say, with all reverence, that you are not learned in the laws of this your Realm of England . . . which is an art which requires a long study and experience before a man can attain to the cognizance of it. The law is the golden met-wand and measure to try the causes of Your Majesty's subjects, and it is by that law that

THE INFLUENCE OF RELIGION ON LAW 49

Your Majesty is protected in safety and peace." King James, in a great rage, said, "Then I am to be under the law—which it is treason to affirm." The Chief Justice replied, "Thus wrote Bracton, 'The King is under no man, save under God and the law.'"

Those words of Bracton, quoted by Coke, "The King is under God and the law," epitomise in one sentence the great contribution made by the common lawyers to the constitution of England. They insisted that the executive power in the land was under the law. In insisting upon this they were really insisting on the Christian principles. If we forget these principles, where shall we finish? You have only to look to the totalitarian systems of government to see what happens. The society is primary, not the person. The citizen exists for the State, not the State for the citizen. The rulers are not under God and the law. They are a law unto themselves. All law, all courts, are simply part of the state machine. The freedom of the individual, as we know it, no longer exists. It is against that terrible despotism, that overwhelming domination of human life, that Christianity has protested with all the energy at its command.

THE PERILS OF INDIVIDUALISM

In noticing, however, the evils of the totalitarian system, let us also remember that individualism has its perils. The Puritans, who insisted that the King was under God and the law, carried their individualism too far, or at any rate, some of their successors did. On the one hand, they had a great sense of the supreme importance of the individual soul and a vital instinct for setting bounds to the State. On the other hand, they held that there was a natural law which gave every man a right to all the property that he could acquire by his own labour, and once having acquired it, he could amass it, increase it and dispose of it as he willed, without any obligation to account to anybody for his stewardship. The great exponent of this individualism was our own philosopher John Locke, who has had more influence on American thought even than he had on English thought. The Constitution of the United States shows one side of the Puritan outlook. It imposes strict limits on the action of those who wield power in the land. The extreme importance attached to the ownershop of property in the United States shows another side of Puritanism.

No one doubts now that it is wrong to treat rights of property as sacred. As Sir Ernest Barker has well said, the individualism of the Puritans "based on religion was made to trail clouds of ingloriousness." There have been many people who, having amassed or inherited property, have only too often forgotten that it is only through society that they have acquired it. They have failed to realize that they are under a duty to use it for the benefit of society as a whole and not for their own material advantage. When rights of property are carried to these lengths they are contrary to all Christian teaching. They disregarded the high duty of unselfishness. As it is said in the First Epistle of St. John (3:17), "But whoso hath this world's goods and seeth his brother have need, and shutteth up . . . his compassion from him, how dwelleth the love of God in him?"

THE INFLUENCE OF CHRISTIANITY

This brings me to the latest and most important influence of Christianity on our law. The preaching of many divines and notably of William Temple brought home the evils of the excessive accumulation of wealth and opportunity in few hands. This has played a considerable part in the great changes in the law. The most important, no doubt, have been made by Parliament which turned us into a Welfare State which recognizes that the State has a duty to secure for every citizen so far as possible full freedom and opportunity for the development of his talents, unhampered by poverty or ill-health. This action by Parliament was reflected in decisions of the Judges, notable in cases relating to employers and workmen. The courts repeatedly emphasized the responsibility of employers to provide safe conditions of work for their workmen and, in case of accident, to compensate them for their injuries. Now this trend has gained further legislative force in recent statutes such as the Health and Safety at Work Act of 1974.

But this new state of society has its dangers. It has brought in its train a great increase in the powers of the central government and a lessening of the authority of Parliament and the Courts, so much so that there are fears that the initiative and enterprise of the individual has been hampered too much. We must hope that this danger can be overcome. It can, I suggest, only be done if we recognize that Christianity is not only a personal religion but also that it has much to teach society itself.

FAMILY LIFE

There is one more subject I must mention, and, in some ways, it is the most important of all. It is the institution of marriage. The Christian Church has always maintained that marriage is a life-long union, for better or worse, so long as both shall live. Divorce was never allowed so as to give the right to remarry. This principle was in marked contrast to other legal systems such as the Jewish laws or the Roman law which always permitted divorce to a greater or lesser extent. The principle of the indissolubility of marriage was in England for centuries not only the law of the Church but also the law of the land. It had a profound influence on the social life of the country. The family is the primary social unit. The well-being of the whole community requires that children should, so far as possible, be brought up by their own parents as members of one family, with all the give and take that family life demands, and also with the security that it affords. The institution of marriage is the legal foundation of this family life. The principle of indissolubility was the binding force which cemented it. Now the State has abandoned this principle, and divorce is easily obtained. The result is that people have come to regard divorce as a matter which can be arranged between the parties. In so doing, they all too often disregard the interests of their children and pursue their own selfish ends. Every thinking person is profoundly disturbed by this state of affairs. It has a grave effect on the family unit and on the national character. It is almost impossible for the State to retrace its steps so as to make the divorce law more difficult. The only real remedy is the growth of a strong public opinion condemning divorce, and, I would add, condemning infidelity. It should not be regarded, as it now is, as the private concern of the parties with which no one else has anything to do. And if the law fails to uphold the institution of marriage, how can we expect young people to do so? Very many now live together, as if married, without bothering to marry at all. No one seems to mind. But so often their associations quickly come to grief. This development is undermining the institution of the family and the whole fabric of society. It even strikes the law itself. These are all matters of great concern to everyone who has the welfare of this country at heart.

CHANGE

But I do not want you to think that I am urging simply that we turn the clock back. Far from it! As I have tried to explain in my book *The Discipline of Law (1979)*, much of our law needs updating. As I wrote there, "The principles of law laid down by the Judges in the 19th century—however suited to social conditions of that time—are not suited to the social necessities and social opinion of the 20th century. They should be moulded and shaped to meet the needs and opinions of today." But that moulding and shaping cannot be left to Parliament alone. All too often it is swayed by the political views of the party in power without reference to any moral basis. In all this lawyers have a special part to play. They can and do exert great influence in Parliament, in the Courts of law, in arbitrations and indeed in all places where people meet to discuss. We must all the time and in every way do all we can to bear witness to the eternal and unchanging truths of our Christian faith.

CONCLUSION

This brings me to the end. And what does it all come to? Surely this, that if we seek truth and justice, we cannot find it by argument and debate, nor by reading and thinking, but only (as our forefathers said) by the maintenance of true religion and virtue. Religion concerns the spirit in man whereby he is able to recognize what is truth and what is justice. Law is only the application, however imperfectly, of truth and justice in our everyday affairs. If religion perishes in the land, truth and justice will also perish. We have already strayed too far from the faith of our fathers. Let us return to it, for it is the only thing that can save us.

Denning
1 May 1989